Art Smart

How to Draw Dinosaurs

Christine Smith

For a free color catalog describing Gareth Stevens' list
of high-quality books and multimedia programs,
call 1-800-542-2595 (USA) or 1-800-461-9120 (Canada).
Gareth Stevens Publishing's Fax: (414) 225-0377.
See our catalog, too, on the World Wide Web: http://gsinc.com

Library of Congress Cataloging-in-Publication Data

Smith, Christine (Christine Hunnikin)
    How to draw dinosaurs / by Christine Smith.
       p. cm. --(Art smart)
    Includes index.
    Summary: Step-by-step instructions for drawing nine different
dinosaurs.
    ISBN 0-8368-1609-9 (library binding)
    ISBN 0-8368-1921-7 (trade)
    1. Dinosaurs in art--Juvenile literature. 2. Drawing--
Technique--Juvenile literature. [1. Dinosaurs in art.
2. Drawing--Technique.] I. Title. II. Series.
NC780.5.S65 1996
743'.6--dc20   95-53869

First published in North America in 1996 by
Gareth Stevens Publishing, 1555 North RiverCenter Drive,
Suite 201, Milwaukee, Wisconsin, 53212, USA.
Original © 1993 by Regency House Publishing Limited
(Troddy Books imprint), The Grange, Grange Yard, London,
England, SE1 3AG. Text and illustrations by Christine Smith.
Additional end matter © 1996 by Gareth Stevens, Inc.

Printed in the United States

3 4 5 6 7 8 9 01 00 99 98

Gareth Stevens Publishing
MILWAUKEE

Materials

Drawing pencils have letters printed on them to show the firmness of the lead. Pencils with an *H* have very hard lead. Pencils with an *HB* have medium lead. Pencils with a *B* have soft lead. Use an *HB* pencil to draw the outlines in this book. Then use a *B* pencil to complete the drawings.

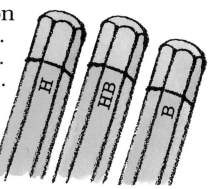

This type of pencil sharpener works well because it keeps the shavings inside a container.

Once you have drawn the outlines on a piece of paper, place a thinner sheet of paper over them. Then make a clean, finished drawing, leaving out any unnecessary lines.

Use a soft eraser to make any changes you might want. Color your drawings with felt-tip pens, watercolors, crayons, or colored pencils.

Shapes

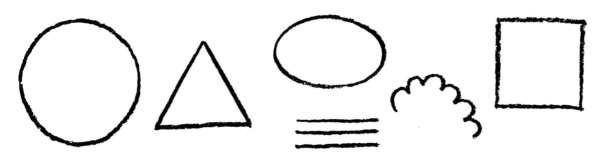

Before you begin drawing, practice the shapes above. Draw them over and over again. All the drawings in this book are based on these simple shapes.

Color

Mixing colors is fun whether you are using colored pencils or paints. Mix red and yellow to make orange. Mix blue and yellow to make green. Red and blue make purple.

To make the dinosaurs you draw seem big, draw any other items in the picture much smaller. From looking at dinosaur bones, scientists have an idea of the sizes and shapes of dinosaurs. But they cannot tell what colors the dinosaurs were or what their skin was like.

If possible, take a trip to the zoo. Look carefully at the lizards and other small creatures like them. Sketch them on paper, and make a note of their colors and any special markings they may have.

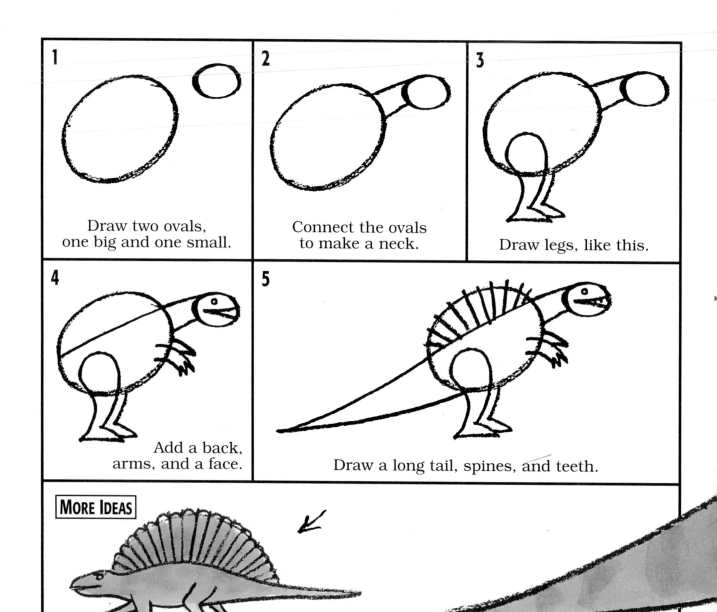

1 Draw two ovals, one big and one small.

2 Connect the ovals to make a neck.

3 Draw legs, like this.

4 Add a back, arms, and a face.

5 Draw a long tail, spines, and teeth.

MORE IDEAS

Spinosaurus had huge spines.

It had needle-like teeth and was a meat eater.

Spinosaurus

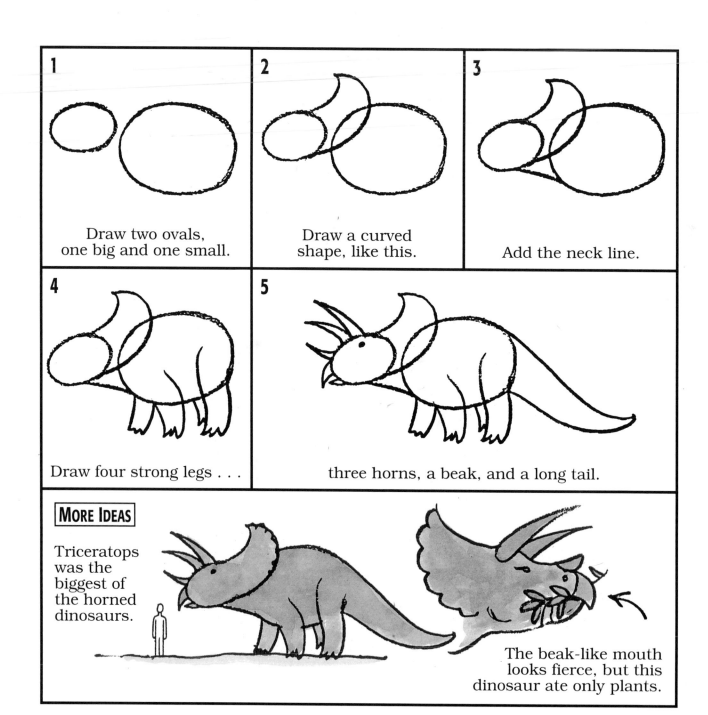

1 Draw two ovals, one big and one small.

2 Draw a curved shape, like this.

3 Add the neck line.

4 Draw four strong legs . . .

5 three horns, a beak, and a long tail.

MORE IDEAS

Triceratops was the biggest of the horned dinosaurs.

The beak-like mouth looks fierce, but this dinosaur ate only plants.

8

Triceratops

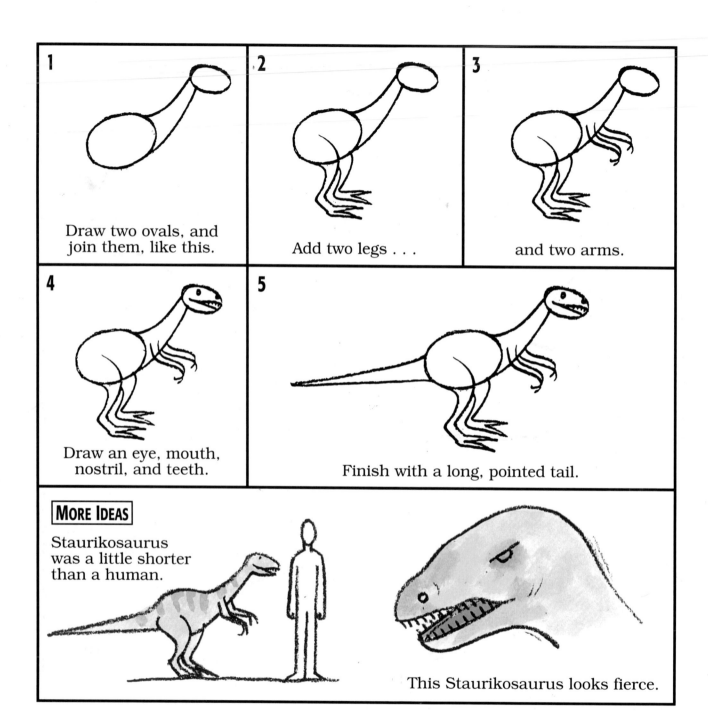

1 Draw two ovals, and join them, like this.

2 Add two legs . . .

3 and two arms.

4 Draw an eye, mouth, nostril, and teeth.

5 Finish with a long, pointed tail.

MORE IDEAS

Staurikosaurus was a little shorter than a human.

This Staurikosaurus looks fierce.

Staurikosaurus

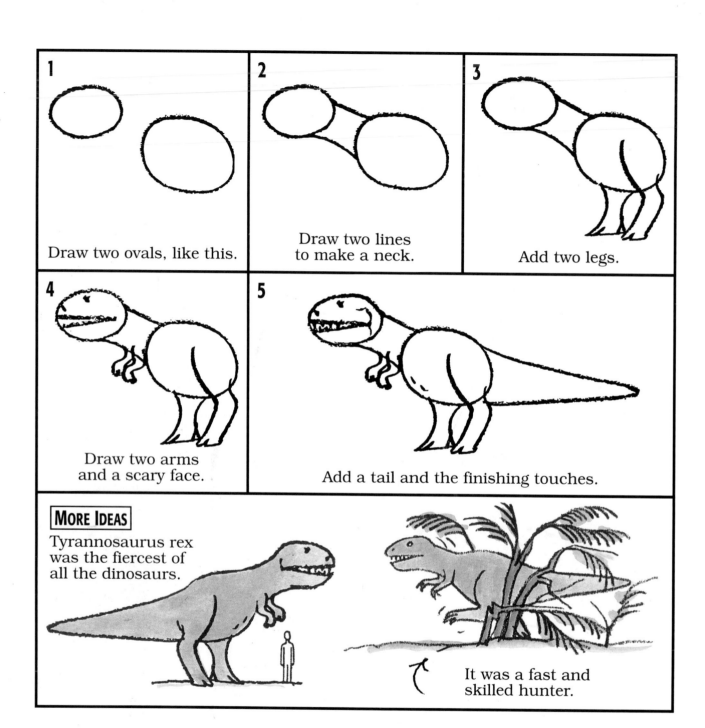

1 Draw two ovals, like this.

2 Draw two lines to make a neck.

3 Add two legs.

4 Draw two arms and a scary face.

5 Add a tail and the finishing touches.

MORE IDEAS

Tyrannosaurus rex was the fiercest of all the dinosaurs.

It was a fast and skilled hunter.

Tyrannosaurus rex

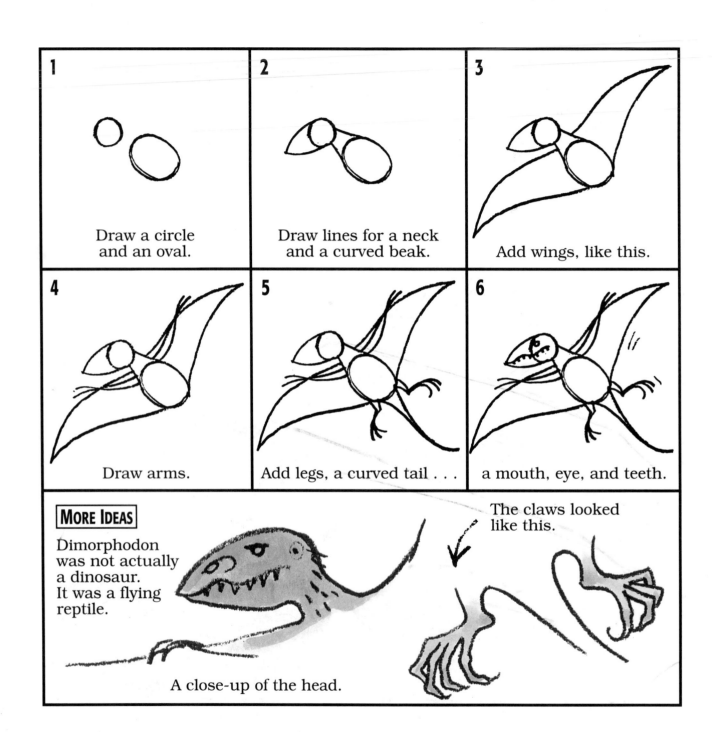

1 Draw a circle and an oval.

2 Draw lines for a neck and a curved beak.

3 Add wings, like this.

4 Draw arms.

5 Add legs, a curved tail . . .

6 a mouth, eye, and teeth.

MORE IDEAS

Dimorphodon was not actually a dinosaur. It was a flying reptile.

A close-up of the head.

The claws looked like this.

Dimorphodon

1 Draw a circle.

2 Then draw this shape.

3 Add legs, like this.

4 Draw a back and tail.

5 Add zigzags down the back.

6 Draw the finishing touches.

MORE IDEAS

Draw a person next to the dinosaur to give an idea of the hugeness of Stegosaurus.

Stegosaurus ate plants.

Stegosaurus

1 Draw two ovals and a circle.

2 Add lines for a neck.

3 Draw legs and arms.

4 Draw in a face.

5 Finish with a pointed tail and a spine, like this.

MORE IDEAS

Ceratosaurus was twice as tall as a human.

It had a short horn on its snout.

Ceratosaurus

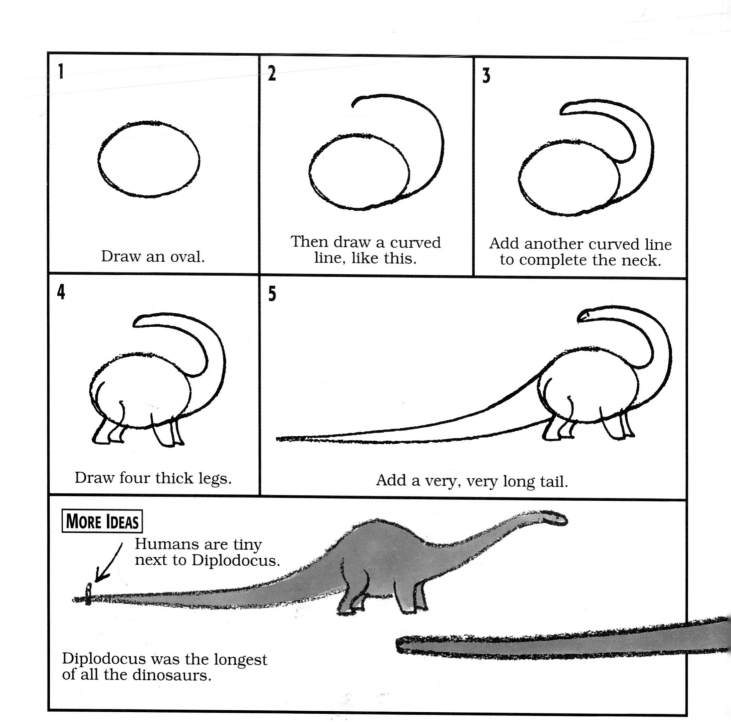

1

Draw an oval.

2

Then draw a curved line, like this.

3

Add another curved line to complete the neck.

4

Draw four thick legs.

5

Add a very, very long tail.

MORE IDEAS

Humans are tiny next to Diplodocus.

Diplodocus was the longest of all the dinosaurs.

Diplodocus

1

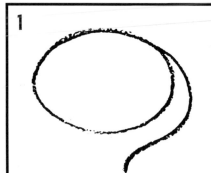

Draw an oval and
a curved line, like this.

2

Add lines for a neck.

3

Draw four thick legs.

4

Draw in a face,
and add sharp spines.

5

Finish with a pointed tail and more spines.

MORE IDEAS

Kentrosaurus
was half as tall
as a human.

It used its sharp spines
for self-defense.

Kentrosaurus

More Books to Read

Animal Crafts. Worldwide Crafts (series). (Gareth Stevens)
Death From Space: What Killed the Dinosaurs? Isaac Asimov (Gareth Stevens)
Dinosaur Hunt! Rolf E. Johnson and Carol Ann Piggins (Gareth Stevens)
Dinosaurs. Michael Benton (Simon & Schuster)
Dinosaurs. David Lambert and Rachel Wright (Franklin Watts)
Discovering Dinosaur Babies. Miriam Schlein (Macmillan)
Draw! Dinosaurs. Doug DuBosque (Peel Productions)
Draw a Dragon Book. Bruce R. Beddow (Vantage)
Draw, Model, and Paint. Drawing Dinosaurs. (Gareth Stevens)
The New Dinosaur Collection (series). (Gareth Stevens)
The New Dinosaur Library (series). Dougal Dixon (Gareth Stevens)

Videos

Animals of the Past. Draw Along (series). (Agency for Instructional Technology)
Art Lessons for Children with Donna Hugh. (Coyote Creek)
Did Comets Kill the Dinosaurs? (Gareth Stevens)
Digging Up Dinosaurs. (Great Plains Instructional Library)
Dinosaur. (Pyramid Film and Video)
Dinosaurs. (Instructional Video)
Dinosaurs and Strange Creatures. (Good Apple)

Index

Ceratosaurus 18-19
colored pencils 2, 3
colors 3, 4
crayons 2

Dimorphodon 14-15
Diplodocus 20-21
drawing pencils 2

eraser 2

felt-tip pens 2

Kentrosaurus 22-23

lizards 4

paints 3
pencil sharpener 2

reptile, flying 14-15

shapes 3, 4
sketching 4
spines 6-7, 18-19, 22-23

Spinosaurus 6-7
Staurikosaurus 10-11
Stegosaurus 16-17

Triceratops 8-9
Tyrannosaurus rex 12-13

watercolors 2
wings 14-15

DAMAGE NOTED

Description: Doodles on
Back page.

Date: Juns/22   Initials: CA
Library: PCML